Digital Building: A Step-By-Step Guide to Accelerate Online Success

MICHAEL BURTON

Table of Contents

Conclusion: Accelerate Your Website Success

Embarking on the entrepreneurial journey is a transformative odyssey, akin to weaving a tapestry where each thread symbolizes a crucial step toward the realization of your clothing website. This section sets the stage for your journey, exploring the essence of starting from nothing and shaping it into something extraordinary.

Just to get started lets dive into a little history of a few well known businesses that exist to give you some clues on how big this opportunity can get you to. You probably already know about this one.

It's Gucci. Gucci was founded in 1921 by Guccio Gucci, started as a small leather goods and luggage company in Florence, Italy. Over the decades, it evolved into a global luxury brand synonymous with sophistication and style. With an annual revenue surpassing $10 billion, Gucci's success lies in its commitment to innovation, quality craftsmanship, and an unwavering dedication to the brand's unique identity being able to be broadcast over the internet has made an even bigger impact for this company allowing people who might not have known about its existence to become aware of it.

Louis Vuitton:

Established in 1854 by Louis Vuitton, this French fashion house initially focused on crafting luxury trunks. Today, Louis Vuitton is a global icon known for its high-end fashion and accessories. With an annual revenue exceeding $15 billion, Louis Vuitton's success lies in its timeless designs, craftsmanship, and an ability to adapt to evolving consumer preferences.

City Trends:

City Trends, a contemporary fashion brand targeting urban youth with affordable, trendy styles, has rapidly risen since its founding. With a keen focus on market trends, City Trends has achieved significant success, with annual revenues surpassing $2 billion. The brand's story underscores the importance of identifying a niche and resonating with a specific audience.

Macy's:

Starting as a small dry goods store in 1858, Macy's has grown into one of the largest department store chains in the United States. Known for its diverse range of products and omnichannel success, Macy's generates annual revenues of over $20 billion. Macy's journey showcases the significance of adapting to changing consumer behaviors and embracing innovation.

Here Are Two Big Entrepreneurial Web Success Stories that have won over many hearts across the internet.

Gary Vaynerchuk:

Renowned entrepreneur Gary Vaynerchuk, founder of VaynerMedia, built his success by leveraging the power of the internet. Starting with his family's wine business, Gary transformed it into a multi-million dollar enterprise through e-commerce and digital marketing. His monthly revenues, driven by a strong online presence, soared to six figures, emphasizing the potential of strategic online ventures.

Sara Blakely:

Founder of Spanx, Sara Blakely revolutionized the fashion industry with her innovative approach to shapewear. Embracing e-commerce, she turned her idea into a billion-dollar business. Sara's monthly revenues skyrocketed, showcasing the impact of combining a unique product with effective online strategies.

This introduction aims to inspire by highlighting the incredible journeys of iconic fashion brands and successful entrepreneurs, setting the tone for your own entrepreneurial adventure.

Defining Your Niche and Brand Identity

Step 1: Self-Reflection and Market Analysis

Begin by reflecting on your passion, values, and unique perspective. Conduct a thorough analysis of the fashion market, identifying gaps and opportunities. Learn from Gucci's approach, understanding how the brand aligned its identity with market demands.

Step 2: Target Audience Identification

Define your target audience by considering demographics, preferences, and lifestyle. Explore City Trends' success in catering to the urban youth. Use this insight to create a persona that embodies your ideal customer.

Step 3: Unique Selling Proposition (USP)

Development

Craft a Unique Selling Proposition that sets you apart.

Analyze Louis Vuitton's success in offering timeless

elegance through quality craftsmanship. Your USP

should resonate with your target audience and align

with your brand identity.

Step 4: Brand Aesthetics and Visual Identity

Translate your brand identity into aesthetics and visual

elements. Consider Macy's approach to diverse market

presence. Select a color palette, logo, and design

elements that reflect your brand's personality.

Step 5: Storytelling and Brand Messaging

Develop a compelling brand story and messaging strategy. Learn from the storytelling techniques employed by successful brands. Share your journey, values, and mission in a way that resonates with your audience.

Step 6: Website Creation from Scratch

Transitioning to building your website, start with selecting a domain name that reflects your brand essence. Follow Gucci's example of a luxurious web address. Choose a reliable hosting platform, and explore website builders like Shopify or WordPress, taking into account your budget and technical expertise.

Step 7: Website Design and User Experience

Design your website with a focus on aesthetics and user-friendliness. Consider Macy's seamless shopping experience. Select a layout, color scheme, and navigation that enhances the overall user experience.

Step 8: Content Creation and Marketing Strategy

Create engaging content that aligns with your brand identity. Leverage social media platforms for marketing, drawing inspiration from City Trends' success on Facebook and Instagram. Utilize storytelling techniques to make your brand narrative compelling.

By the end of this section, you will have a well-defined niche, a unique brand identity, and a functioning website that reflects your vision. These actionable steps, illustrated by the success stories of industry leaders, will empower you to navigate the complexities

of defining your niche and establishing a compelling

brand presence online.

CHAPTER 2

Creating a Domain Name for Your Website Instructions

Creating a memorable and meaningful domain name is a crucial step in establishing your online presence. Here's a step-by-step guide on how to do it using two popular website platforms—WordPress and Shopify—both of which allow you to have ownership over your domain name.

Step 1: Research and Brainstorm

Start by researching your niche and understanding your target audience. Consider the essence of your brand and the message you want to convey. Brainstorm keywords, phrases, and combinations that align with your brand identity. Think about the uniqueness and memorability of the potential domain names.

Step 2: Check Availability

Once you have a list of potential domain names, check their availability. You can use domain registration platforms or tools provided by hosting services. For WordPress, you can use a domain registrar like Namecheap or GoDaddy. For Shopify, you can check domain availability directly within the Shopify platform.

Step 3: Choose a Platform

Decide whether you want to use WordPress or Shopify for your website. Both platforms offer flexibility and control over your domain.

WordPress:

If you choose WordPress, select a reliable hosting provider. Popular options include Bluehost, SiteGround, and HostGator.

Sign up for a hosting plan that aligns with your website's needs.

During the registration process, you'll have the option to choose and register your domain name. Follow the platform's prompts to enter your chosen domain.

Shopify:

If you prefer Shopify, sign up for a Shopify account.

In the Shopify dashboard, go to "Online Store" and then "Domains."

Here, you can either buy a new domain or connect an existing one. If you're buying a new domain, Shopify will guide you through the process.

Step 4: Domain Registration and Ownership

Complete the domain registration process. Fill in your contact information and billing details. Review the registration terms and policies to ensure you understand them.

WordPress:

After completing the registration, you'll have full ownership of your domain. Ensure that the domain is registered in your name, providing you with control and flexibility.

Shopify:

If you're buying a new domain through Shopify, the domain will be automatically registered in your name. If connecting an existing domain, follow Shopify's instructions to update the DNS settings with your domain registrar.

Step 5: Configure Domain Settings

Once your domain is registered, configure the domain settings to point to your website.

WordPress:

In your hosting provider's dashboard, navigate to the domain management section.

Configure the domain settings to point to your WordPress website. This typically involves updating the domain's DNS records.

Shopify:

In the Shopify dashboard, go to "Online Store" and then "Domains."

Configure the DNS settings as instructed by Shopify. This step ensures that your domain is correctly linked to your Shopify store.

Step 6: Secure Your Domain

Consider enabling domain privacy protection to keep your personal information confidential. This service is often offered by domain registrars and helps protect against spam and identity theft.

By following these steps on WordPress or Shopify, you'll successfully create and own a domain name for your website. Remember, a well-chosen domain name enhances your brand identity and contributes to the overall success of your online venture.

CHAPTER 3

Creating a One-Click Funnel for Ecommerce: A Step-by-Step Guide

Creating a one-click funnel for an ecommerce website involves streamlining the user journey, making the purchasing process as seamless as possible. Here's a guide on how to implement a one-click funnel using two popular platforms—Shopify and WordPress (with WooCommerce).

Shopify:

Install a Shopify App:

In your Shopify admin, go to the "Apps" section.

Click on "Visit the Shopify App Store" and search for one-click checkout apps like "OneClickUpsell" or "Zipify OneClickUpsell."

Install and configure the app according to your preferences.

Configure One-Click Upsells:

Set up upsell offers that appear after a customer makes a purchase with one click. This could include complementary products, special discounts, or limited-time offers.

Customize the appearance and messaging of your upsell to maximize effectiveness.

Enable One-Click Checkout:

Ensure that your checkout process is optimized for one-click purchasing. Simplify the checkout form and remove unnecessary steps.

Integrate with payment gateways that support one-click checkout, such as Shopify Payments or third-party providers compatible with one-click functionality.

Test and Optimize:

Run tests to ensure the one-click funnel is functioning smoothly. Analyze customer behavior and adjust upsell offers based on data.

Monitor conversion rates and continuously optimize the one-click checkout process for better results.

WordPress (WooCommerce):

Install a WooCommerce Extension:

Navigate to your WordPress dashboard and go to "Plugins."

Click on "Add New" and search for a one-click checkout plugin like "WooCommerce Quick Checkout."

Activate and Configure:

Install and activate the chosen plugin.

Configure the plugin settings, including design elements and user experience preferences.

Set Up One-Click Upsells:

Use a plugin like "WooCommerce One Click Upsell Funnel" to create post-purchase upsell offers.

Define your upsell strategy, such as offering related products, upgrades, or discounts.

Simplify Checkout:

Optimize the standard WooCommerce checkout

process by removing unnecessary fields and steps.

Enable guest checkout to reduce friction for first-time

customers.

Integrate with Payment Gateways:

Ensure your chosen payment gateway supports one-

click checkout. Popular options like Stripe and PayPal

often have native support for seamless transactions.

Test and Refine:

Conduct thorough testing to ensure the one-click funnel

is working as expected.

Gather user feedback and make adjustments based on

customer experience and preferences.

Remember to comply with privacy and security standards when implementing one-click checkout, and always communicate the benefits of the process to your customers to enhance trust and transparency. Regularly monitor analytics to refine and optimize the one-click funnel for improved conversion rates.

CHAPTER 4

In this section it will explain what an ecommerce website and accelerator program is and how to use it for your advantage.

E-commerce Website:

An e-commerce website is an online platform that facilitates the buying and selling of goods or services over the internet. It provides businesses with a digital storefront to showcase their products, enabling customers to browse, select, and purchase items conveniently. E-commerce websites come in various forms, from small boutique shops to large-scale marketplaces, and they play a crucial role in the modern retail landscape. Here are key components and considerations for leveraging an e-commerce website:

Product Listings:

Clearly display your products or services with high-quality images, detailed descriptions, and pricing information.

Shopping Cart:

Enable users to add items to their cart for easy checkout, mimicking the traditional shopping experience.

Secure Payment Gateways:

Integrate reliable and secure payment options to ensure smooth transactions and build trust with customers.

User Accounts:

Allow users to create accounts to track orders, save preferences, and facilitate a personalized shopping experience.

Mobile Responsiveness:

Ensure your website is optimized for mobile devices to capture the growing segment of mobile shoppers.

Search Engine Optimization (SEO):

Implement SEO strategies to improve the visibility of your website on search engines, driving organic traffic.

Customer Reviews and Ratings:

Incorporate a system for customer reviews and ratings to build credibility and aid other shoppers in their decision-making process.

Shipping and Returns:

Clearly communicate shipping options, costs, and

return policies to manage customer expectations and

satisfaction.

Analytics:

Utilize analytics tools to track user behavior, identify

trends, and make data-driven decisions to enhance the

overall user experience and optimize conversions.

Accelerator Program:

An accelerator program is a structured and time-limited

business development initiative designed to help

startups and early-stage companies grow rapidly. These

programs provide entrepreneurs with resources,

mentorship, networking opportunities, and often

funding in exchange for equity. Here's how you can

leverage an accelerator program to your advantage:

Access to Mentors:

Accelerators connect you with experienced mentors

who provide valuable guidance and insights, helping

you navigate challenges and make informed decisions.

Networking Opportunities:

Joining an accelerator introduces you to a network of fellow entrepreneurs, industry experts, and potential investors, expanding your professional connections.

Educational Resources:

Accelerator programs typically offer workshops, seminars, and training sessions to enhance your business knowledge and skills.

Funding:

Many accelerators provide seed funding or investment opportunities, giving your startup the financial boost it needs to accelerate growth.

Validation:

Being accepted into an accelerator program acts as a stamp of approval, providing validation to potential investors, partners, and customers.

Structured Timeline:

Accelerators follow a structured program with specific milestones, pushing you to achieve measurable progress within a defined timeframe.

Demo Days:

Most accelerator programs conclude with a demo day, where startups pitch their businesses to a room full of investors, potential partners, and industry experts, increasing visibility and opportunities for funding.

CHAPTER 5

How to Use Integration of E-commerce with the

Accelerator Support to Your Advantage.

Leverage the mentorship and educational resources of

the accelerator to fine-tune your e-commerce strategy.

Use the network gained through the accelerator to

establish partnerships, collaborations, and potential

customer relationships for your e-commerce business.

Funding for E-commerce Growth:

Seek funding opportunities offered by the accelerator to

invest in marketing, technology enhancements, or

expanding your product range on your e-commerce

platform.

Validation for Investors and Customers:

Highlight your participation in an accelerator program

on your e-commerce website. This serves as a powerful

validation, building trust with potential investors and

customers.

Strategic Planning and Optimization

Apply the knowledge gained from the accelerator

program to strategically plan and optimize your e-

commerce operations, from website design to

marketing strategies.

Networking for E-commerce Expansion:

Leverage the accelerator's networking opportunities to

connect with industry leaders, potential customers, and

collaborators who can contribute to the growth of your

e-commerce business.

Iterative Improvement:

Use the accelerator program's structured timeline to implement iterative improvements to your e-commerce website. Regularly assess and refine your strategy based on the insights gained.

By combining the power of an e-commerce website with the resources provided by an accelerator program, you can create a synergistic approach to accelerate the growth of your online business. The mentorship, funding, and network gained through the accelerator can significantly contribute to the success and scalability of your e-commerce venture.

Now you will learn how to create your own accelerator program to improve your website step by step guide. Creating your own accelerator program to improve your website involves careful planning, resource allocation, and a structured approach. Here's a step-by-step guide to help you establish an effective accelerator program for website improvement:

Step 1: Define Program Objectives and Goals

Clearly outline the objectives of your accelerator program. Are you aiming to boost website traffic, enhance user experience, increase conversions, or achieve a specific business milestone?

Set measurable goals to track the success of the accelerator, such as a percentage increase in website engagement or a decrease in bounce rates.

Step 2: Identify Areas for Improvement

Conduct a comprehensive audit of your website to identify areas that need improvement. This may include website design, user interface, content quality, page load speed, and overall functionality.

Step 3: Develop a Structured Timeline

Establish a timeline for the accelerator program, including specific milestones and deadlines. This will help create a sense of urgency and structure for participants.

Step 4: Build a Mentorship Network

Recruit experienced mentors from your industry who can provide guidance and expertise to participants. Ensure that mentors have a track record of success in areas relevant to website improvement.

Step 5: Define Selection Criteria for Participants

Clearly outline the criteria for selecting participants.

Consider factors such as the current state of their

websites, their commitment to the program, and the

potential for positive impact.

Step 6: Create an Application and Selection

Process

Develop an application process that gathers relevant

information about each participant's website and their

goals for improvement.

Establish a selection committee or panel to review

applications and select participants based on the defined

criteria.

Step 7: Provide Resources and Tools

Identify and provide necessary resources, tools, and

technologies that participants can use to enhance their

websites. This may include access to design software, analytics tools, and development resources.

Step 8: Offer Educational Workshops and Training

Organize workshops and training sessions led by industry experts to educate participants on best practices for website improvement. Cover topics such as SEO, user experience design, content creation, and analytics.

Step 9: Facilitate Networking Opportunities

Create opportunities for participants to network with mentors, fellow participants, and other industry professionals. Networking can lead to valuable collaborations and partnerships.

Step 10: Implement a Demo Day or Showcase Event

Conclude the accelerator program with a demo day or showcase event where participants present the improvements made to their websites. Invite potential investors, industry leaders, and other stakeholders to attend.

Step 11: Collect and Analyze Feedback

Gather feedback from both participants and mentors to evaluate the effectiveness of the accelerator program. Use this feedback to make improvements for future iterations.

Step 12: Recognize and Reward Success

Acknowledge and reward participants who have achieved significant improvements in their websites.

Recognition can include certificates, featured profiles, or other incentives.

Step 13: Iterate and Improve

Reflect on the outcomes of the accelerator program and identify areas for improvement. Use insights gained to refine the program structure, content, and overall effectiveness for future iterations.

By following these steps, you can create a tailored accelerator program that focuses on improving specific aspects of your website. This initiative not only enhances your website but also provides valuable learning experiences for participants and fosters a collaborative community within your industry.

ABOUT THE AUTHOR

"SUCCESS LOVES SPEED"

www.ingramcontent.com/pod-product-compliance
Lightning Source LLC
Chambersburg PA
CBHW070224260726
48658CB00006BA/2150